Original title:
Midnight Frost

Copyright © 2024 Swan Charm
All rights reserved.

Author: Olivia Oja
ISBN HARDBACK: 978-9916-79-609-2
ISBN PAPERBACK: 978-9916-79-610-8
ISBN EBOOK: 978-9916-79-611-5

Frost's Tender Touch on Sleeping Earth

Morning whispers soft and clear,
Frost's embrace holds me near.
Nature sleeps in silver lace,
Dreams unfold in gentle grace.

Each blade shines with icy glow,
Secrets wrapped in winter's show.
Harmony in chilly air,
Awakening beyond compare.

Trees don crystal crowns so bright,
Guardians of the tranquil night.
Beneath the stars, they stand tall,
Whispers echo, nature's call.

Crystalline Footprints of the Night

Moonlight dances on the ground,
Crystalline footprints abound.
Each step tells a tale of grace,
Of wanderers in this vast space.

Silence wraps the world so tight,
Guiding lost dreams through the night.
Stars blink softly, a guide divine,
Leading hearts on paths that shine.

The night air shimmers with delight,
Echoes of laughter take flight.
Beneath the cloak of midnight sky,
Wonders awaken, spirits fly.

Secrets Carved in Frozen Breath

Amidst the frost, stories sleep,
Secrets carved in silence deep.
Whispers float on winter's breath,
Painted dreams in hues of death.

Each exhale etches in white,
Moments captured in the night.
Nature's brush creates a song,
In stillness, where we belong.

Echoes linger in the cold,
Tales of warmth, both new and old.
Within each flake, a memory waits,
A tapestry that love creates.

Beneath the Glistening Canopy

In forest deep, the frost does gleam,
Beneath the trees, a silent dream.
Each branch holds a world of ice,
A wondrous realm, serene and nice.

Glistening jewels adorn the leaves,
Whispers of nature, gentle thieves.
Life sparkles under frosted grace,
Currents hidden in this place.

Underneath the canopy high,
Hope flickers like a firefly.
Together, we find peace in cold,
Wrapped in beauty, brave and bold.

Twilight's Breath on a Canvas of Ice

A whisper dances on the chill,
Where twilight drapes the world in blue.
The breath of dusk begins to thrill,
As starlit dreams fall soft anew.

The frozen lake reflects the glow,
Of fading light in violet skies.
Each flake a secret, drifting slow,
With night's embrace where silence lies.

Stars twinkle like diamonds bright,
Against the backdrop, cold and deep.
They twirl and spin in gentle flight,
While nature wears her cloak of sleep.

In shadowed hearts, the quiet hums,
Of stories left in winter's art.
The canvas speaks, as twilight comes,
And paints the night in every heart.

Echoes of Night's Gentle Caress

Whispers float on velvet air,
A melody of dreams unreal.
Each note a warmth, a soft despair,
In twilight's hush, we learn to feel.

The moonlight bathes the world in peace,
As stars align in vast ballet.
With every breath, the shadows cease,
And night unfolds in sweet array.

Cascades of light on drifting clouds,
Brush echoes where the heart does roam.
Each thought resounds in gentle crowds,
Inviting all to find their home.

The breeze a lover's softest sigh,
Caressing leaves that dance for joy.
In whispers rich, the world will lie,
As night holds tight her precious toy.

Shadows of the Snow-clad Dreamer

Through silver woods the shadows play,
On carpet white, they twist and weave.
The dreamer walks in soft array,
A path of wonder, hearts believe.

Each snowflake tells a tale of old,
Of whispered wishes, lost in time.
The world adorned in purest gold,
A fleeting moment, like a rhyme.

In silence deep, the echoes call,
As starlit tales begin to glow.
The dreamer, wrapped in nature's thrall,
Explores the depths where few will go.

Frosted breath upon the night,
Illuminates the soul's own quest.
In shadows soft, the heart takes flight,
A dance with dreams, forever blessed.

Frosted Petals Beneath the Starlight

In gardens kissed by winter's breath,
The petals gleam in icy light.
Each bloom a whisper, soft as death,
Embraced by moonbeams, cold and bright.

Beneath the stars, they bow their heads,
In reverence to the night so dear.
Each frozen tear, the silence spreads,
While dreams alight, and hopes appear.

A portrait framed in crystal hues,
Reveals a world of hidden grace.
From every flake, a heart renews,
Awakening the night's embrace.

The frost-infused petals softly sigh,
In harmony with twilight's tune.
Beneath the vast and endless sky,
Their beauty speaks of life in June.

Secrets of the Frozen Twilight

Whispers of night in chilly air,
Frosted dreams beyond compare.
Silence drapes the world in white,
  Secrets shimmer in the light.

Stars peek through the icy shroud,
  Veils of mist, softly bowed.
  In the woods, shadows play,
    Keeping warmth at bay.

Moonlight dances on the stream,
  Frozen echoes of a dream.
Nature holds her breath in awe,
Capturing beauty, pure and raw.

Glistening Shadows of Late Hour

In the stillness, night unfolds,
Glistening secrets, softly told.
Shadows flicker, dance with grace,
In the twilight's gentle embrace.

Cold winds whisper through the trees,
Echoes carried by the breeze.
Stars twinkle in a velvet sky,
Painting dreams as moments fly.

Crystal leaves on branches sway,
Holding memories of the day.
With every glimmer, time stands still,
Capturing hearts with quiet thrill.

Eclipsed by Frost's Embrace

Underneath the moonlit glow,
Frost wraps all in purest snow.
Nights so cold, yet spirits soar,
Finding warmth in nature's lore.

Whispers travel on the air,
Tales of beauty everywhere.
Eclipsed by frost, the world lies still,
Nature's breath, serene and chill.

Glistening trails on frozen lakes,
Holding secrets, stillness wakes.
In this magic, time stands still,
Frost's embrace, a quiet thrill.

Twilight's Frigid Caress

As twilight falls with gentle hand,
A frigid caress across the land.
Stars ignite in the darkened dome,
Guiding wanderers safely home.

Every flake, a story spun,
Winter's canvas, pure and fun.
Shimmering roads of silver bright,
Lead us deeper into night.

In the cold, dreams intertwine,
Seeking solace, hearts align.
Twilight's chill wraps us tight,
Embracing peace until the light.

Nightfall's Shimmering Cloak

The sun descends with fading light,
Wrapped in shadows, the world takes flight.
Stars emerge, a silent vow,
Whispers painted on night's brow.

A gentle breeze begins to sing,
Caressing the trees, as night takes wing.
Moonlit paths of silver grace,
Each step reveals a hidden place.

A tapestry of dreams unfolds,
In twilight's touch, the heart beholds.
Secrets linger, softly spun,
In dusk's embrace, the world is one.

From distant hills, the night calls near,
With every echo, whispers clear.
Through starlit eyes, the night is bright,
In awe, we bask in gentle light.

Wrapped in nightfall's shimmering cloak,
Each breath, a spell, as shadows spoke.
In this realm where dreams unite,
The beauty breathes, the heart takes flight.

Twinkling Fragments of a Frozen Sky

Above the world, the cosmos gleams,
With tiny stars that weave our dreams.
Each twinkle holds a tale untold,
A fragment of the night so bold.

In frozen silence, beauty reigns,
Across the dark, a dance of chains.
Stars like diamonds, finely cast,
In winter's grasp, the die is fast.

The hush of night invites the soul,
To wander where the spirits stroll.
Hearts align with cosmic flow,
In starlit paths, we come to know.

The Milky Way, a river bright,
Leads us through the boundless night.
In this expanse, we find our place,
Amidst the light, in endless space.

Twinkling fragments whisper low,
The universe's timeless glow.
In frozen skies, our hopes arise,
With every twinkle, we realize.

Veils of Ice in the Stillness

A crystal world in slumber lies,
Beneath the weight of silent skies.
Veils of ice embrace the trees,
Draped in winter's cool decrees.

The breath of frost, a fleeting chill,
Paints the landscape, quiet, still.
Each branch adorned, a sparkling sight,
In perfect harmony with night.

Snowflakes dance like whispered dreams,
Falling softly, or so it seems.
They weave a quilt of purest white,
A gentle warmth in winter's bite.

The stillness speaks in hushed sounds,
Where nature's peace forever abounds.
In icy hands, the world holds tight,
The secrets of the chilly night.

Veils of ice, soft and clear,
Guard our thoughts; the spark we steer.
In stillness, we embrace the grace,
Of winter's touch in time and space.

Serenade of the Frosty Night

Underneath a blanket deep,
Stars awaken from their sleep.
A serenade of cold and light,
Echoes softly through the night.

Gentle whispers in the air,
Frosty songs without a care.
The moon hums a lullaby,
As shadows dance and dreams fly high.

A symphony of nature plays,
In the frozen night's embrace.
Each note drifts upon the breeze,
Carried through the silent trees.

The world transformed, a wondrous sight,
Wrapped in calm, the heart takes flight.
In this realm of silver gleam,
We find ourselves lost in a dream.

Serenade of the frosty night,
Guides the hearts that seek the light.
With every breath, the world awakes,
In harmony, the stillness shakes.

The Chilled Sighs of a Winter's Night

The moonlight dances on the snow,
Whispers of wind, soft and low.
Trees stand silent, cloaked in white,
Ghostly shadows fade from sight.

Stars twinkle in the darkened sky,
While the world breathes a gentle sigh.
Frosted whispers fill the air,
Nature's stillness, beyond compare.

Footprints crunch upon the ground,
Echoes of the night resound.
In this realm, time holds its breath,
A tapestry woven with apparent depth.

Firelight flickers, warm and bright,
Inviting dreams of soft delight.
Under blankets, snug and tight,
The chilled sighs of a winter's night.

Beneath the Glint of the Celestial Sphere

In the stillness of the night,
Stars paint stories, pure and bright.
Galaxies swirling, vast and grand,
Whispers echo across the land.

The moon hangs low, a silver crest,
Beaming softly, a quiet guest.
Under her gaze, dreams take flight,
Beneath the glint of the celestial sphere.

Constellations sing ancient songs,
Guiding the lost, where one belongs.
With every twinkle, wishes bloom,
In the tapestry of endless gloom.

The night unfolds its vast embrace,
Filling hearts with gentle grace.
Underneath the starlit quilt,
Hope awakens, never stilt.

Tranquil Nights in Frost's Tender Hold

The night is wrapped in frosty dreams,
Moonlit shadows weave their seams.
Frosted whispers in the pines,
Nature hums its quiet lines.

Stars adorn the velvet sky,
While the world rests, soft and shy.
Every breath a cloud of mist,
In this moment, nothing missed.

Gentle silence hugs the trees,
Carried softly on the breeze.
Footsteps muffled, soft and light,
In tranquil nights of winter's bite.

Wrapped in warmth, the hearth aglow,
Outside the chill, a world of snow.
In frost's tender hold, we find,
Peaceful solace for the mind.

A Tapestry of Frosted Hues

Amidst the canvas, white and blue,
A tapestry of frosted hues.
Nature brushes with quiet grace,
Winter's charm, a soft embrace.

Icicles dangle from the eaves,
Jewel-like sparks on frozen leaves.
Every flake a story told,
In a winter's night, fierce and bold.

With every breath, the world transforms,
In the stillness, magic forms.
The crisp air, a call to roam,
In frosted beauty, we find home.

Silence reigns, a gentle peace,
In this winter's sweet release.
Each moment savored, pure and true,
A tapestry of frosted hues.

Whispers Beneath the Crystal Canopy

Beneath the branches' heavy weight,
Soft murmurs float, a gentle fate.
The twilight sings, in shadows deep,
While nature sighs, and whispers keep.

A secret dance in chilly air,
Frosted leaves with tender care.
Stars peek down with twinkling eyes,
As dreams weave through the starry skies.

Echoes of laughter fill the night,
The world transformed in silver light.
A hush blankets the sleeping earth,
Cradling all in its serene hearth.

With every breath, the silence sways,
A fleeting chill that gently stays.
Whispers echo in the still,
Under the canopy, hearts fulfill.

Embrace the magic, soft and sweet,
In this sanctuary, time's retreat.
In frozen wonders, life unfolds,
A symphony of stories told.

Serenade of the Icy Branches

In the stillness, silence reigns,
A serenade of icy chains.
Branches bow with heavy grace,
Nature's touch in cold embrace.

Moonlight dances on the frost,
Whispering dreams that won't be lost.
Each flake's descent, a note, a tune,
Gliding softly, beneath the moon.

Chiming quietly in the night,
Winter's spirit, pure delight.
A symphony, so calm, serene,
Woven in the silver sheen.

Winds caress with gentle breath,
A lullaby of life and death.
In this moment, time stands still,
Echoing through the silent chill.

Serenely wrapped in crystal light,
Nature's song, the world ignites.
Each heartbeat beats a little slow,
As icy branches sway and flow.

The Sleep of Eternal Winter

In a world where silence grows,
Eternal winter softly flows.
A blanket pure, so white and deep,
The forest falls into its sleep.

Frosted dreams on every tree,
Drifting slow, as time agrees.
Night cradles all in gentle care,
Wrapped in stillness, dreamers stare.

Thoughts like snowflakes softly land,
Muffled whispers, gentle hand.
The heart of winter beats so slow,
Embracing all in moonlit glow.

Sleepy echoes fill the air,
A tranquil peace beyond compare.
Every breath, a sigh of cold,
In the dreamscape, tales unfold.

On this canvas, pure and bright,
The stars weave stories through the night.
Eternal beauty holds its ground,
In the peace of silence found.

Glacial Dreams in a Moonlit Realm

In a realm of glacial grace,
Moonlight paints each frozen place.
Dreams take flight on wings of ice,
Whispers dance, a paradise.

Stars like diamonds, bright and clear,
Guide the night with gentle cheer.
A tapestry of cool delight,
Shimmers softly, pure, and bright.

Each breath, a cloud, ephemeral,
Stories rise, invincible.
With every heartbeat, night unfolds,
In the glacial dreams it holds.

Crystalline echoes gently sing,
Of distant lands and winter's wing.
A serenade, in shadows vast,
Binding futures with the past.

As dawn approaches, dreams abide,
In the serenity, we confide.
Glacial whispers fill the air,
In moonlit realms, we find our share.

The Quiet Pulse of a Cold Night's Heart

In the stillness, whispers flow,
Beneath the blanket of soft snow,
Stars flicker like distant dreams,
The world holds its breath, or so it seems.

Moonlight drapes a silver sheen,
Glistening over the evergreen,
A gentle hush in the air,
Nature's symphony laid bare.

Crickets hush, the owls call,
Echoes rise and softly fall,
Each heartbeat, a rhythmic beat,
A serenade where night and calm meet.

Shadows stretch, both long and deep,
In this moment, time does sleep,
Wrapped in quiet, there's a spark,
The night pulses softly in the dark.

With every sigh, the cold draws near,
A solace that we hold most dear,
Together in the night we wander,
In the pulse of peace, we ponder.

Moon's Reflection on the Breath of the Earth

Silent waters catch the glow,
Waves whisper softly, rise, and flow,
The moon spills silver on the sea,
A tranquil dance, wild and free.

Clouds drift like thoughts across the sky,
Brushstrokes of dreams that float and fly,
Each ripple tells a tale unheard,
Nature's poetry, softly stirred.

In the coolness, shadows glide,
The earth breathes deep, in grace, it hides,
Roots entwined beneath the ground,
Whispers of life all around.

Branches sway in the gentle breeze,
Caressing leaves with tender ease,
The moon keeps watch, a patient guide,
Reflecting love from far and wide.

Time rests here in this quiet scene,
Where Earth and sky remain serene,
In every glance, beauty defined,
In the moon's embrace, peace we find.

Between the Stars and Ice

Frozen dreams on winter's breath,
Stars shimmer, whispering of death,
In a world where silence reigns,
Crystals dance on windowpanes.

Night wraps the earth in a gentle cloak,
Each breath a cloud, the stillness spoke,
Ice-laden branches twist and bend,
In the night, where shadows blend.

Between the stars, a path outlined,
Leading souls to what they find,
In the void, warmth resides,
With every twinkle, joy abides.

Frosted whispers greet the dawn,
As the stars fade, the light has drawn,
Canvas painted in hues of gold,
Stories of the night retold.

Holding close this tranquil night,
In the silence, find the light,
Between the stars and ice we tread,
With hope igniting paths ahead.

Beneath a Glistening Blanket

Soft flakes dance on winter's breath,
Covering the earth, a silent death.
Glistening jewels twinkle bright,
A frosty shimmer under starlight.

Each step crunches, crisp and clear,
Nature whispers, drawing near.
Peaceful stillness fills the air,
In this wonder, we share a prayer.

Branches bend with heavy lace,
Nature's grace in pure embrace.
Underneath the shining sheet,
The world transforms, a quiet seat.

In the hush, we find our dreams,
Flowing as the soft moonbeams.
Whirling thoughts, like snowflakes swirl,
In this magic, hearts unfurl.

Beneath the blanket, secrets lie,
Awaiting spring, beneath the sky.
The glistening world awaits the thaw,
In every flake, a silent awe.

The Stillness of Frozen Time

In quiet realms where shadows play,
The moments linger, softly sway.
Frozen whispers fill the air,
Time stands still; we breathe, we care.

Frosted glass, reflections gleam,
In silence, we awaken dreams.
The clock ticks on, yet here we stay,
In frozen beauty, we'll not stray.

Echoes of the past reside,
In every tear, the tides abide.
A stillness that transcends the day,
In frozen time, we find our way.

Moments cherished, held so tight,
In a world draped soft in white.
Stillness wraps around our soul,
A pause in time, we feel whole.

And when the thaw returns anew,
We'll dance again, me and you.
But for now, let silence chime,
In the stillness of frozen time.

Beneath a Glistening Blanket

Soft flakes dance on winter's breath,
Covering the earth, a silent death.
Glistening jewels twinkle bright,
A frosty shimmer under starlight.

Each step crunches, crisp and clear,
Nature whispers, drawing near.
Peaceful stillness fills the air,
In this wonder, we share a prayer.

Branches bend with heavy lace,
Nature's grace in pure embrace.
Underneath the shining sheet,
The world transforms, a quiet seat.

In the hush, we find our dreams,
Flowing as the soft moonbeams.
Whirling thoughts, like snowflakes swirl,
In this magic, hearts unfurl.

Beneath the blanket, secrets lie,
Awaiting spring, beneath the sky.
The glistening world awaits the thaw,
In every flake, a silent awe.

The Stillness of Frozen Time

In quiet realms where shadows play,
The moments linger, softly sway.
Frozen whispers fill the air,
Time stands still; we breathe, we care.

Frosted glass, reflections gleam,
In silence, we awaken dreams.
The clock ticks on, yet here we stay,
In frozen beauty, we'll not stray.

Echoes of the past reside,
In every tear, the tides abide.
A stillness that transcends the day,
In frozen time, we find our way.

Moments cherished, held so tight,
In a world draped soft in white.
Stillness wraps around our soul,
A pause in time, we feel whole.

And when the thaw returns anew,
We'll dance again, me and you.
But for now, let silence chime,
In the stillness of frozen time.

Lingering Shadows of Winter's Glow

As daylight fades, shadows wane,
The crisp air holds a gentle strain,
Winter casts its silent spell,
In the hush, we know it well.

Fires crackle, warmth alive,
In quiet corners, spirits strive,
With every flicker, hearts aglow,
Among the lingering winter's flow.

Footprints marked in soft white sheen,
Trace the paths where we have been,
Each step a moment held so dear,
In the glow, we shed our fear.

The twilight rustles, softly calls,
A tapestry where silence falls,
Each star above, a wish to send,
As the night whispers, shadows blend.

Hold this time, let moments linger,
With the glow of warmth in each finger,
In winter's grasp, we find our way,
Through shadows deep, to a brighter day.

Echoes of a Cool Embrace

Whispers of the night surround,
Softly in the stillness found.
Each breeze carries tales untold,
In shadows where the dreams unfold.

Hearts wrapped in the moon's warm glow,
In moments where the echoes flow.
A dance of silence, pure and free,
In every sigh, a memory.

Gentle breezes brush the skin,
Inviting thoughts to deep within.
Nature's calm, a sweet reprieve,
In cool embraces, we believe.

Stars above, in twinkling grace,
Guide us through this misty space.
In every breath, a promise lives,
In stillness, all the heart forgives.

Echoes linger, soft and light,
Fading into the gentle night.
With every heartbeat, we partake,
In cool embraces, fears will break.

Luminescent Imprints on the Ground

In the twilight's gentle glow,
Footprints sparkle, soft and slow.
Wishes whispered on the breeze,
Carved in shadows, hearts at ease.

Glimmers trace the path we walk,
In every step, the stars do talk.
Guiding lights through lonely night,
Imprints shining, pure delight.

Each moment echoes, bright and rare,
In luminescence, love laid bare.
A journey shared, hand in hand,
As starlit trails adorn the land.

Through fields of dreams, we wander free,
With glowing footprints, you and me.
Memories bright, forever last,
Imprints of the future, held fast.

In light and shadow, paths entwine,
In every step, our hearts align.
Together, under the moon's embrace,
In luminescent, sacred space.

Night's Caress in a Crystal Clutch

In twilight's embrace, shadows creep,
Stars blink and twinkle in silence deep.
Moonlight drapes like whispered lace,
A tranquil world in soft, dark space.

Frosted whispers on the air,
Glistening gems beyond compare.
Each breath a shimmering sigh,
As dreams of starlight drift and fly.

Glimmers dance on the cheek of night,
Awaking hearts with muted light.
Through dreams we wander, soft and slow,
In a cradle where shadows glow.

The world feels wrapped in velvet calm,
Each moment sweet, a soothing balm.
In night's soft clutch, the heart finds peace,
While worries fade and troubles cease.

With every star that finds its place,
Night breathes life, a warm embrace.
In crystal clutch, we drift away,
To realms where night and dreams will play.

When Faeries Dance on Frosted Grass

When morning breaks with a silver hue,
Dewdrops shimmer, wildflowers too.
Whispers of laughter lift the air,
As faeries twirl without a care.

Misty veils waft soft and bright,
Sunbeams weave through joyous light.
With each step, their magic sways,
Enchanting hearts in playful ways.

Crickets pause to hear their tune,
Nature hums a morning croon.
Petals blush with delight anew,
In dances shared, both swift and true.

Around the glow of daisies fair,
Beyond the brook, they leap with flair.
Joyous notes fill the frosted morn,
While shadows stretch, and new dreams are born.

With laughter echoing all around,
In whispered secrets, magic's found.
When faeries dance, the world feels light,
A wondrous spell beneath the sunlight.

The Sigh of Winter's Stillness

Amidst the hush where silence reigns,
Winter settles, soft like chains.
With every breath, the world feels near,
In icy moments, calm and clear.

Frosted panes weave intricate lace,
Time seems caught in delicate grace.
The whispering winds softly sigh,
While winter's secrets drift and lie.

Branches bow with sparkling weight,
Nature's beauty, still, sedate.
In the heart of this frozen spell,
Every flake a tale to tell.

Footsteps muffled, echoes fade,
In white blankness, dreams are laid.
The world may slumber, deep and low,
But in its heart, a glow does grow.

With every dawn, a promise glows,
In winter's sigh, a warmth bestows.
As fleeting moments come to rest,
In stillness, find what we love best.

Glimmers of White in the Shaded Grove

In the grove where shadows meet,
Glimmers of white beneath my feet.
Softly lays the tranquil snow,
Whispers of winter ebb and flow.

Branches weave a frosted dome,
Nature's arms, a sheltering home.
In the hush of this sacred place,
Thoughts drift softly, time finds grace.

Dappled light through leaves allah,
Casts gentle patterns like a song.
The world is hushed, a sacred art,
In stillness, nature speaks to heart.

Snowflakes dance in a waltz of chill,
Turning air to a gentle thrill.
Beauty blooms in the frosted air,
A tranquil moment, quiet, rare.

Each breath I take brings peace anew,
In glimmers white, the heart feels true.
In the grove's embrace, I find my place,
A bond with nature, a soft grace.

Glacial Dusk's Gentle Touch

Whispers of cool winds flow,
As shadows start to grow.
The sky wears a bruised hue,
While stars peek softly through.

Mountains cradle the twilight,
Embracing the fading light.
Silence drapes the cold earth,
A canvas of waning mirth.

Crystals sparkle on the frost,
In this beauty, none are lost.
Nature's breath still and slow,
In glacial dusk's soft glow.

The moon casts a silver smile,
Bringing calm like a warm isle.
Beneath its watchful gaze,
The world slips into a daze.

Embers of the sun now fade,
Night's embrace, a tender aid.
In this moment, all is right,
A lullaby of soft night.

Silver Veils of the Night

Softly falling, silver light,
Cloaks the world in tender night.
Stars like whispers, brightly weave,
Tales that shimmering leaves.

Glistening paths around me sway,
Guiding dreams that drift away.
Moonbeams dance on quiet streams,
Entwined within the night's dreams.

Each shadow holds its secret song,
In the dark, where we belong.
Branches sway with gentle grace,
Kissing earth in a warm embrace.

The cool air breathes with thought,
Threads of magic, softly caught.
In this silver-touched expanse,
Every heart begins to dance.

Nighttime whispers, truth unfolds,
Wrapped in light, the world beholds.
A tapestry of dreams in sight,
Woven deep in silver night.

Secrets Encased in Icicles

Hanging low from eaves so high,
Icicles trap the winter sky.
Beneath their shimmer, worlds lie still,
Secrets held with icy will.

Whispers of the past reside,
Frozen tales too shy to glide.
Crystal chains that bind the air,
Reflecting stories, rare and rare.

In the stillness, echoes roam,
Ancient hearts find their way home.
Icicle tears of skies weep,
Guardians of the dreams we keep.

Every drop a moment lost,
Chilling pathways, whispers tossed.
In their beauty, time stands still,
Nature's breath, a gentle thrill.

As the sun begins to rise,
Icicles shimmer, caught in sighs.
They melt away the secrets held,
In sunlight's warmth, dreams dispelled.

Lullabies of the Frosty Air

Gentle breezes kiss the pines,
Singing songs of winter's lines.
While soft snow blankets the earth,
Kindling dreams of warm rebirth.

Each flake a note in nature's tune,
Whirling softly, morning's boon.
Frosty whispers drift and sway,
In the twilight, dreams will play.

Clouds of silver softly glide,
Wrapped in starlight, winter's pride.
In the hush, the world finds peace,
As the frosty air's embrace.

The moon hangs low, a guardian bright,
Guiding dreams in the velvet night.
With every breath, a story flows,
In lullabies, the heart knows.

Crickets cease their nightly hum,
In this stillness, we become.
Cradled in the frosty air,
The world sings softly, free from care.

Silent Shimmers of the Night

Stars twinkle high, a silent sigh,
In velvet skies, secrets lie.
Whispers of dreams dance and play,
As night unfolds, shadows sway.

Moonbeams kiss the earth so light,
Crafting tales in the hush of night.
Each echo holds a hidden song,
In the dark, where we belong.

The breeze carries tales of old,
Of love, of loss, and hearts so bold.
Quiet moments weave their thread,
In tranquil realms where fears are shed.

A silver glow on tranquil streams,
Guides us softly into dreams.
Nature breathes a hymn so sweet,
In the stillness, our souls meet.

Here in silence, time stands still,
Embraced by night, we feel its will.
In the quiet, hearts ignite,
As we dance through silent night.

Crystal Whispers in the Dark

Each droplet gleams, a crystal tear,
Whispers flutter, soft and clear.
In shadows deep, where secrets dwell,
The night holds tales it cannot tell.

Beneath the stars, a silence hums,
Echoing softly, the past becomes.
Voices of night, so sweetly spun,
In the dark, our souls are one.

Glimmers of light, like fleeting dreams,
Bathe the world in silver streams.
In this quiet, we find our grace,
As shadows dance, we find our place.

The hush of night, a sacred space,
Cradles thoughts in its warm embrace.
Every sigh, a story we share,
In crystal whispers, we dare to care.

In the depths of dark, hope will arise,
With every flicker, a promise lies.
Together we walk, hand in hand,
In this tranquil, enchanted land.

Veil of Winter's Embrace

Snowflakes fall like whispered vows,
Blanketing earth with hushed brows.
Each flake a secret, soft and white,
Within the calm of winter's night.

Branches bare, cloaked in frost,
Nature's beauty never lost.
A stillness reigns, serene delight,
In the heart of the winter's light.

Footsteps crunch on powdered ground,
In this silence, peace is found.
Every breath, a puff of haze,
In winter's chill, our hearts ablaze.

Stars peep through the frosty veil,
Telling stories of love's trail.
In the night's crisp, we find our way,
Guided by moonlight's gentle sway.

Wrapped in warmth, the world retreats,
In winter's embrace, our spirit beats.
Through chill and quiet, we shall sing,
For in cold heart, warmth takes wing.

Luminous Crystals on Silent Paths

Crystals glint in morning's light,
Sparkling on the ground below.
Every step a soft delight,
As winter's magic starts to glow.

Footprints upon a silvery track,
Leading forth to wonders bright.
Nature whispers, never slack,
Guiding souls with sheer delight.

Trees adorned with icy lace,
Embrace the morning's gentle kiss.
In this still and sacred place,
Every breath a frozen bliss.

Wander on this path of dreams,
Where the heart finds peace anew.
Life unfolds in glistening streams,
Underneath the sky so blue.

When Darkness Meets the Whiteness

When shadows stretch across the land,
  And whiteness blankets all in sight.
  Two worlds merge, a gentle hand,
    Twilight fading, chasing night.

Frosted breath hangs in the air,
  Whispers soft in twilight's gloom.
  Beauty lingers everywhere,
  In the dance of night's perfume.

Footsteps echo down the way,
  Lost in realms where silence dwells.
  In darkness, light finds its play,
  As winter's magic softly swells.

Hope and fear entwined as one,
  Underneath the crescent glow.
  In this game, the day is done,
  As shadows in the soft light flow.

Secrets Wrapped in Winter's Breath

Whispers carried on the breeze,
Secrets held in crystal hush.
Nature paints with gentle ease,
In the quiet, hearts will rush.

Beneath blankets of pure white,
Dreams will dance in frozen air.
All the world a wonderland,
Wrapped in snow, beyond compare.

Footprints trail where stories sleep,
Every flake a tale to tell.
In this moment, shadows creep,
While winter casts its icy spell.

Amidst the chill, a warmth ignites,
Fireflies of memory glow.
Winter's heart, soft and polite,
In the depths of frost and snow.

Frost-laden Fables of the Night

In the quiet of snow, tales arise,
Whispers of frost under darkened skies.
Shadows dance on the glistening white,
Echoes of dreams in the still of night.

Branches adorned with a delicate lace,
A touch of magic, a tranquil embrace.
Carried by wind, secrets unfold,
Stories of warmth in the bitter cold.

The moon casts its glow on the silent ground,
In every flurry, soft tales are found.
In the heart of winter, the fables sing,
Of love and hope, and the joys they bring.

With every breath, a cloud of mist,
Memories linger in the frost's sweet kiss.
In the tapestry bright, colors collide,
Frost-laden fables where dreams abide.

So gather your tales, let them ignite,
In the depths of cold on this magical night.
For every whisper in the frosty air,
Is a promise of warmth, if you dare to care.

Whispers of the Chill on the Breeze

Through the trees, a soft sigh flows,
Whispers of chill where the cold wind blows.
Every leaf shivers, a story to share,
Of winter's secrets carried with care.

Beneath the stars that twinkle and gleam,
The night wraps us in a silvery dream.
With the frost painting pictures so bright,
Each breath a poem in the still of the night.

As shadows deepen, the world slows down,
In the hush of white, no fear nor frown.
Nature's embrace, a soothing refrain,
Whispers of chill, like a soft falling rain.

Among the drifts where the cold winds play,
Echoes of warmth refuse to decay.
Held in the grip of a frosty caress,
Lies the heart of winter, tenderly blessed.

So listen closely to the breeze that sighs,
For within each whisper, a magic lies.
Let the chill envelop, like a gentle glove,
And feel the spirit of winter's love.

The Enchantment of Cold Dreams

In the quiet of night, where shadows creep,
Cold dreams awaken, from winter's deep.
Glittering stars on a blanket of gray,
Guide the lost souls who wander away.

With each breath of ice, a vision appears,
Carved of crystal and woven with fears.
Yet hope flutters softly, like wings in the dark,
A flicker of light, a warm little spark.

Under the blanket of silence and snow,
The enchantment of dreams begins to grow.
Nestled in folds, where the chill can't reach,
Magic awakens, as nature will teach.

Each frozen whisper a secret to find,
In the cradle of darkness, a prayer refined.
The beauty of cold, the solace it brings,
Wrapped in the stories that winter sings.

So let your heart dance in the frost and freeze,
Breathe in the magic that lingers with ease.
For in cold dreams, lies a comforting grace,
An enchanting journey through time and space.

Beneath the Spell of Winter's Twilight

As daylight fades, a spell is cast,
In the arms of winter, shadows are vast.
Beneath the twilight, soft whispers flow,
A world transformed by the moon's gentle glow.

In the hush of the night, the air turns bright,
With delicate frost, a shimmering sight.
The trees wear gowns of crystal and lace,
Enchanted by night's cool, tender embrace.

Every breath shared with the chill in the air,
Carries the warmth of love's heartfelt care.
Frozen landscapes tell tales of the past,
In the winter's twilight, memories last.

Stars twinkle softly, like wishes on high,
Their light weaving dreams in the peaceful sky.
Under this spell, where silence reigns free,
Whisper your hopes to the night's reverie.

As dawn approaches, with a light so pure,
In winter's still hold, we forever endure.
Beneath the spell of this magical night,
Hope twirls with grace, wrapped in the twilight.

Secrets Encased in Crystal Silence

Whispers echo through the frost,
Hidden truths at any cost.
Glistening shards in the pale light,
Guarding dreams held out of sight.

Silent figures dance and sway,
Memories trapped in ice's play.
Each breath held in a frozen clasp,
Secrets lost, we dare not grasp.

In the stillness, shadows creep,
Through the crystal, silence weep.
Ancient tales lay intertwined,
In the heart of the frost, confined.

The moon casts light on brittle glass,
As fleeting moments slowly pass.
In the quiet, we may find,
The echoes of what's left behind.

Should you listen to the air,
You'll hear stories, whispers rare.
In crystal silence, shadows gleam,
Guarding tightly every dream.

Embrace of the Frozen Silhouette

In twilight's chill, shadows blend,
Ghostly forms around me bend.
Each silhouette, a tale untold,
Frozen hearts in the icy cold.

With every breath, the world holds still,
Nature's pulse, a silent thrill.
A dance of frost on the silent night,
Stars like candles, burning bright.

Secret paths that lead us far,
Guided by a distant star.
The embrace of winter's hold,
Whispers of the brave and bold.

In the void where silence sleeps,
Ancient promises the darkness keeps.
A figure wrapped in mist and haze,
Lost in memories of frozen days.

Hold me close in your embrace,
A fleeting warmth in this cold space.
Together we can brave the night,
In silhouettes, we find our light.

Night's Enchantment in a Chilling Dream

In the depths of evening's veil,
Where shadows weave a haunting tale.
The shimmering stars blink above,
Casting whispers of silent love.

A chilling breeze sweeps through the trees,
Carrying secrets on the freeze.
Each breath a cloud in the night's embrace,
A dance of dreams in the cosmic space.

In slumber's hold, visions flow,
Through frozen lands where spirits go.
A tapestry of dark and light,
Guiding lost souls through the night.

Enchantments laced with icy beams,
Every heartbeat sings of dreams.
The moon, a guardian in our quest,
Cradles the night as we find rest.

With every sigh, the stars align,
In the chill, our fates entwine.
Let us wander where shadows gleam,
In the night's enchantment, we dare dream.

Surrendering to the Icy Whisper

A hush falls over snowy lands,
Softly forming winter's strands.
Whispers carried on the breeze,
Echoing through the frozen trees.

With every step, the frost will cling,
In silence, hear the icebirds sing.
Their notes like crystals in the air,
Enchant the heart that dares to care.

Surrender to the quiet night,
Where every star is pure delight.
The glacier's breath, a ghostly sigh,
Calls us forth as we drift by.

In every flake, a story sleeps,
In icy whispers, the moment leaps.
Snowflakes twirl like delicate notes,
On whispered winds, the world still floats.

As shadows grow and daylight wanes,
And twilight bathes the land in chains,
We find solace in winter's touch,
Surrendering to the frost, so much.

A Tapestry Woven in Ice

In the chill of dawn's embrace,
Silvery threads weave their trace.
Nature's beauty, pure and bold,
A story in each flake retold.

Crystals dance upon the ground,
Whispers of the frost abound.
Every glimmer, every shine,
Captures warmth in winter's spine.

Pine trees dressed in icy crowns,
A tranquil hush in frozen towns.
Sunlight glimmers, soft and bright,
A tapestry of pure delight.

Flakes descend in silent flight,
Creating landscapes, pure and white.
Layers built with frosty care,
A woven quilt beyond compare.

As night falls, the stars appear,
A frozen world, serene and clear.
Underneath the moon's soft glow,
The ice-bound beauty starts to show.

Frosted Fairytales of the Night

Underneath a blanket white,
Dreams unfold in pure moonlight.
Every crystal tells a tale,
Of whispered winds and secret trails.

Icicles hang like ancient lore,
Guardians of the snowy floor.
Sparkling tales of yore and bliss,
Melt into the starry kiss.

In the woods where shadows play,
Frosted branches gently sway.
Beneath the stars, a story starts,
A fairytale in frosted hearts.

Nighttime's blanket wraps so tight,
Embracing all in soft twilight.
Magic lingers in the air,
In frozen whispers, dreams do flare.

As the dawn begins to rise,
Frosted dreams turn to the skies.
Every tale, a gentle sigh,
In winter's arms, we softly lie.

Flickers in the Frostbitten Air

A breath of winter, crisp and clear,
Flickering lights begin to appear.
Dancing flames in the frosty glow,
A symphony where cold winds blow.

Each glimmer whispers of the night,
Casting warmth, a soft delight.
Beneath the stars, the world enchants,
Frostbitten air in gentle chants.

In this realm of icy dreams,
The moon reflects on silver streams.
Crackling fires with stories old,
A warmth that winter can't withhold.

Winding paths through snowy lanes,
Hold the magic that remains.
Flickers of hope in frozen breath,
Entwined with echoes of the depth.

As the sky begins to change,
Nature's wonders rearrange.
In the stillness, hearts will soar,
Flickers in the frost beg for more.

Starlight's Kiss on Ice-bound Waters

A tranquil lake, a frozen sheet,
Starlight's kiss where waters meet.
Glowing softly in the night,
Reflecting dreams in shimmers bright.

Gentle whispers of the breeze,
Bring forth secrets from the trees.
Underneath the velvet sky,
Ice-bound waters hold their sigh.

Every ripple tells a tale,
Of secret journeys through the veil.
Stars above like lanterns shine,
Guiding hearts in paths divine.

Moonlight dances on the ice,
A silver glow, a paradise.
In this moment, time is still,
The world awakens to the chill.

As night unfolds its dark embrace,
Reflections shimmer, soft and lace.
On ice-bound waters, dreams collide,
Where starlight's kiss cannot hide.

Breath of the Winter Whisper

Cold winds brush against the trees,
Carrying whispers with ease.
Each flake dances in the night,
Embracing all with pure delight.

Frozen lakes and frosty ground,
In silence, magic can be found.
Gentle breaths of winter's air,
Wrap the world in dreams so rare.

Moonlight shimmers on the snow,
Guiding hearts where dreams may go.
A tranquil spell that enchants,
While the icy moment grants.

Stars above, a twinkling song,
Bidding winter to stay long.
Nature sleeps beneath the chill,
Waiting for the sun to thrill.

A quietude that calms the mind,
In winter's breath, peace we find.
With every whisper, every sigh,
The world just pauses to comply.

Crystal Dreams Beneath the Stars

In twilight's grasp, the dreams take flight,
Whispers echo in the night.
Stars like crystals gleam so bright,
Guiding wishes, pure delight.

The cool breeze carries secrets old,
Stories of dreams yet to unfold.
In the stillness, hearts ignite,
Chasing shadows, taking flight.

Reflections dance on moonlit streams,
Awakening our hidden dreams.
Each twinkle holds a tale to share,
In the magic of the air.

As galaxies weave their gentle glow,
We find the paths where dreams may flow.
In every heart, a spark of light,
Inviting us to dream tonight.

So close your eyes and take a chance,
Under the stars, join in the dance.
In every glance, a world of hope,
Crystal dreams help us elope.

Enchanted Silhouettes in the Darkness

Shadows stretch beneath the trees,
Whispers float upon the breeze.
In the dark, silhouettes sway,
Painting dreams in shades of gray.

Mysterious forms softly twirl,
Dancing in a twilight whirl.
Night unveils its tender charms,
Cocooned in nature's gentle arms.

Glimmers peek from stars above,
Wrapping the night in silent love.
Embers spark like fleeting light,
Guiding souls through this still night.

A symphony of whispers play,
In the shadows, night's ballet.
With every breath, the magic flows,
In this realm, where enchantment grows.

So let us wander, hand in hand,
Through the darkness, dreams unplanned.
In silhouettes, our stories blend,
An enchanted night that won't end.

Night's Ethereal Lace

In the hush of twilight's grace,
Night unfurls its delicate lace.
Stars are stitched in velvet skies,
Whispers of the moon arise.

A tapestry of dreams takes form,
Cradled in the night's soft warm.
Each sparkling thread, a tale to weave,
In night's embrace, we dare believe.

Gentle breezes kiss the earth,
Carrying secrets of rebirth.
As shadows dance in elegant flow,
The heart discovers all it knows.

Ethereal patterns, waltzing light,
Drawing us deeper into night.
In this moment, time suspends,
As the universe makes amends.

So linger here, in silence rare,
Let night's lace weave dreams to share.
With every star, a hope ignites,
In the beauty of these endless nights.

Nocturnal Silence in a Crystal World

In the silence of the night,
The moon casts its silver light.
Stars are twinkling, bright and bold,
Whispers of dreams yet untold.

Frosty air wraps around tight,
Shimmering like diamonds bright.
Nature sleeps in peaceful sway,
Waiting for the break of day.

Footsteps crunch on icy ground,
In this world, no other sound.
Echoes of a distant call,
As shadows stretch and softly fall.

Beneath the trees, a soft sigh,
As breezes gently drift by.
A canvas painted black and white,
In this silence, pure delight.

The crystal world holds us near,
Wrapped in beauty, calm, and clear.
Nocturnal whispers fill the air,
In this moment, none compare.

Ethereal Glow of Winter's Grasp

The morning sun breaks through the chill,
Casting hues on snow-covered hills.
An ethereal glow starts to rise,
Painting the world in soft disguise.

Boughs hang heavy with icy gems,
Nature dressed in silver hems.
Each flake that falls tells a tale,
Of winter's magic, strong and frail.

Footprints mark paths in the snow,
A quiet journey, moving slow.
Breath fogs in the crisp, clear air,
A moment captured, pure and rare.

Whispers of frost dance on the breeze,
As trees sway gently, bending knees.
The glow of winter's soft embrace,
Brings warmth to the coldest space.

The world transforms in chilled delight,
Under winter's vivid sight.
In every corner, beauty sleeps,
As the essence of silence keeps.

Awakened by a Chilling Breeze

A stirring breath from distant lands,
Brushes softly against my hands.
Awakened by a chilling gale,
Nature's breath tells its own tale.

Leaves rustle with a gentle sigh,
As clouds drift slowly through the sky.
In this moment, life feels true,
Awakened by the ether's view.

The world is wrapped in a cool embrace,
Every shadow finds its place.
Each sound distinct, each whisper clear,
In this stillness, I hold dear.

Frosty tendrils touch my skin,
As the day's warmth starts to thin.
A dance of light and shadow plays,
In the twilight's fleeting rays.

Embracing change as seasons shift,
In nature's hands, we feel the gift.
The chilling breeze brings forth the night,
Awakening dreams with gentle light.

Frost-kissed Dreams Beneath the Stars

Beneath the stars, the world is still,
Frost-kissed dreams on windowsill.
A blanket of white covers the ground,
In this serenity, bliss is found.

Night wraps all in a calming hush,
As time pauses in the gentle rush.
Dreams entwined with the frosty air,
A moment cherished, bright and rare.

Moonlight dances on frozen streams,
Reflecting back our silent dreams.
Every glimmer, every shade,
Shadows of hopes the night has made.

The universe whispers secrets old,
In patterns of silver and gold.
Embraced by the night's gentle sway,
We find our footprints fade away.

As dawn approaches, we remain,
Treasuring each fleeting gain.
Frost-kissed dreams under celestial seas,
A lullaby carried on the breeze.

Luminescent Veins of a Winter Landscape

Snowflakes flutter in the air,
Beneath the sky's cold stare.
Silence wraps the sleeping trees,
Whispers carried by the breeze.

Icicles hang like crystal tears,
Muffled laughter, hidden fears.
Footprints trace the trails of night,
Guiding hearts towards the light.

Stars emerge in velvet skies,
Painting dreams that never die.
Frosted patterns on the ground,
Nature's beauty, softly found.

A lantern glows, a beacon bright,
Illuminating winter's night.
Each shadow dances, sways, and bends,
In the hush where magic ends.

Beneath the moon's embrace so pale,
Whispers echo on the trail.
In the stillness, time stands still,
Life unfolds by winter's will.

Echo of the Frosted Twilight

Muted hues in dusky light,
The day sighs into the night.
Crisp air tinged with smoky dreams,
Twilight's veil softly redeems.

Stars awake with gentle grace,
Painting silence, an endless space.
Footfalls light on frostbit ground,
In the stillness, peace is found.

Whispers dance in twilight's glow,
Carried where the soft winds blow.
Night unfurls her velvet cloak,
While the world around us wakes and chokes.

Time suspends in this embrace,
Caught within an endless space.
Reflections shimmer in the stream,
The night cradles every dream.

Nature breathes, her secrets shared,
In the moments, hearts laid bare.
Echoes linger in the dark,
As twilight paints its lovely mark.

Glacial Touch on Quiet Paths

Nature sleeps beneath the snow,
While soft whispers start to flow.
Gentle winds caress the trees,
Speaking secrets with the breeze.

Moonlight kisses every peak,
A silver touch, soft and sleek.
Paths of ice, a crystal trail,
Echoes of a winter's tale.

Frozen rivers gleam like glass,
Holding dreams as moments pass.
Footprints linger, tales untold,
In the stillness, hearts grow bold.

Frosty patterns lace the night,
Whispers mingling, pure delight.
Nature sighs, a gentle breath,
As the world finds rest in death.

Stars blink softly high above,
Filling the silence with their love.
The glacial touch, a fleeting grace,
Marks the beauty of this place.

Fractured Reflections of the Night Sky

In the hush of evening's call,
Stars begin their silent fall.
Mirror lakes reflect the light,
Fractured whispers of the night.

Shadows blend in twilight's embrace,
Each twinkle finds its rightful place.
Dreams collide with stardust bright,
Painting stories in the night.

Constellations weave their lore,
Tales of love and wars of yore.
In the depths, the cosmos sighs,
A dance of fate beneath the skies.

Starlights scatter, soft and clear,
Filling hearts with hope and cheer.
Night unveils her endless guise,
In the cosmos, wisdom lies.

Every star a tale to share,
Fractured reflections, dreamers' prayer.
The sky beckons, vast and wide,
As the night becomes our guide.

Crystal Moonlight on Still Waters

Beneath the stars, the waters gleam,
Reflections dance, a silver dream.
Whispers soft as night unfolds,
A tranquil tale in silence told.

The moonlight plays with shadowed hue,
A gentle kiss, the world anew.
Ripples sigh in soft embrace,
As cosmic wonders find their place.

Crickets sing their serenade,
In harmony, the night won't fade.
Each flicker paints a story bright,
In crystal moonlight's tender light.

The world reclines in peaceful hush,
While time drifts gently in its rush.
Every breath brings calm and peace,
As nature weaves its sweet release.

In quietude, the heart finds home,
Beneath the sky, forever roam.
With each reflection, love will sway,
In stillness, find the dawn of day.

The Yearning of Chilled Air

Breath of winter, crisp and clear,
Whispers echoes, far and near.
The world in white, a stunning sight,
Yet hearts remember summer's light.

Trees stand bare against the blue,
As skies wear gray, a somber hue.
Each gust carries a silent plea,
For warmth, for sunlight, for the sea.

Footsteps crunch on frosty ground,
In solitude, a quiet sound.
The yearning stirs within the soul,
For golden days that once were whole.

Yet in the chill, hope flickers bright,
Like distant stars in silent night.
The promise of spring waits to bloom,
In every breath, dispelling gloom.

As seasons shift, the heart will know,
In every chill, the warmth will grow.
For all that fades must also bloom,
In winter's breath, life's sweet perfume.

Embraced by the Winter's Breath

Snowflakes fall, a gentle touch,
Nature whispers, soft as such.
Wrapped in layers, cozy tight,
We find comfort in the night.

Fires crackle, warmth emerges,
In the glow, the heart surges.
With every sip of cocoa warm,
We feel the snows' enchanting charm.

Children play in fields of white,
Laughter echoes, pure delight.
Every snowman, every sled,
Is born from dreams in ice and red.

Footprints carved in fresh terrain,
Tell the stories, joy and pain.
The brisk embrace of winter's grace,
Invites us all to find our place.

As nights grow long and days turn gray,
We cherish moments, come what may.
In winter's hold, we find our song,
Together here, where we belong.

Traces of Frost in the Night's Song

Silent night wrapped in soft shroud,
Stars above like jewels, proud.
Frosted windows catch the gleam,
Of moonlight's glow, a silver stream.

Each breath released in chilly air,
Is like a whisper, light as prayer.
Echoes linger, soft and low,
As nature's art begins to show.

The quiet hum of distant roads,
Beneath the weight of winter's loads.
The world is still, a canvas pure,
A tranquil heart, a timeless cure.

In the distance, shadows play,
As nighttime dreams begin to sway.
The crispness bites, yet hearts are warm,
In the night's song, we find our form.

Traces of frost caress the dark,
In every twinkle, life's sweet spark.
In harmony with the stars above,
We live in wonder, we breathe in love.

Footprints in a Frozen Moment

In the snow, a path unfolds,
Silent tales the winter holds.
Each step whispers of the past,
Frozen echoes, memories cast.

Nature brushes with its chill,
Time stands still on yonder hill.
Footprints blend in twilight's glow,
A fleeting dance where moments flow.

Beneath the sky, so vast and bright,
Dreams take flight in frosty light.
In this instant, life feels real,
Each heartbeat, every breath we feel.

The air is crisp, the world adorned,
In this peace, our souls are warned.
For as we walk, the sun will rise,
Yet here we pause, beneath the skies.

In footsteps soft, our stories blend,
Through winter's grasp, our hearts transcend.
A frozen moment, brief yet clear,
In whispered winds, we draw you near.

Resilience of the Winter Night

Under the stars, the cold does bite,
Yet hearts ignite, strong in the night.
Chill winds may howl, shadows may fall,
Still, we rise through it all.

The moonlight glimmers on the frost,
In every loss, there's hope embossed.
Through stormy skies, we brave the dark,
A flicker of strength, a resilient spark.

Each breath we take writes a new page,
In the rhythm of winter, we find our stage.
In the silence, we hear the call,
Of nature's beauty, enchanting all.

Beneath the shroud of chilly air,
We find warmth in the bonds we share.
For in the night, together, we stand,
Crafting futures, hand in hand.

Resilience blooms in the barren land,
Hope threads through like fine-woven sand.
In the depths of night, dreams take flight,
Embracing the chill with all our might.

Beneath the Shimmering Dome

Under the heavens, a soft light glows,
Stars like whispers, secrets they show.
The sky adorned in shimmering lace,
Inviting all to pause and embrace.

A canvas vast, where dreams ignite,
Guided gently by the moon's soft light.
Beneath this dome, we share our dreams,
In sight of wonders, life truly gleams.

In every twinkle, stories unfold,
Of journeys taken, of hearts made bold.
The night wraps us in its gentle embrace,
A sacred space, a timeless place.

Together we dance under cosmic tides,
With the universe, our spirit abides.
Beneath the shimmer, we find our part,
In this vastness, we heal the heart.

So let us wander where stardust flows,
Beneath the dome, our love only grows.
In every sigh, in every gaze,
We find connection in the winter's haze.

Celestial Mists on a Frosty Eve

As twilight falls, the mists arise,
Veiling earth beneath starry skies.
A breath of magic cloaks the night,
In frosty air, everything feels right.

Each step we take, a dance with dreams,
Where silence whispers, joy redeems.
Through the fog, we find our way,
In the heart of winter, we choose to stay.

The world transforms in gentle grace,
Every shadow finds its place.
In the cool embrace of night's soft sighs,
Life's simple pleasures softly arise.

With every moment wrapped in white,
Celestial wonders, a pure delight.
In this scene, our worries cease,
Within each heartbeat, we find our peace.

So let us cherish this frosty eve,
With every star, we dare to believe.
In celestial mists, our spirits soar,
Through winter's grasp, we long for more.

Glimpses of a Winter Reverie

Snowflakes whisper soft and light,
As twilight dances with the night.
Frosty breath upon the pane,
Dreams of warmth in winter's reign.

Stars like diamonds, cold and bright,
Guide the wanderers through the night.
A hush descends, the world at rest,
In winter's heart, we feel so blessed.

Branches dressed in silvery lace,
Nature dons its purest face.
Footprints fade on glittered ground,
In this stillness, peace is found.

Candles flicker, shadows play,
Memories of a sunlit day.
Through the chill, the warmth will flow,
In a reverie, love will grow.

As morning dawns with rosy hue,
Promises of life feel fresh and new.
The winter's song, a soft farewell,
In every heart, its magic dwells.

A Dance Among the Ice Crystals

In the glade where silence reigns,
Ice crystals twinkle, nothing pains.
Each flake twirls in frosty air,
A dance of beauty, light, and flair.

Branches sway with gentle grace,
Nature's waltz in a frozen place.
The moon beams down on silver snow,
Whispers of winter softly flow.

The stars align, a twinkling show,
As shadows glide and soft winds blow.
A ballet of frost, pure delight,
In this realm of purest white.

Chill wraps round like a lover's kiss,
Enfolding dreams in icy bliss.
Every breath like smoke and sighs,
Underneath the wintry skies.

With every spin, the world stands still,
Nature's heart, a vibrant thrill.
In this dance where time suspends,
The spirit soars and winter lends.

Echoes in the Hushed Cold

Whispers float on frosty air,
Echoes of a world laid bare.
Every sound is soft and low,
Where secrets of the cold winds blow.

Footsteps crunch on a quilt of white,
Through the woods, into the night.
Nature paints with quiet grace,
Creating dreams in frozen space.

The frozen lake, a mirror bright,
Reflects the stars, a wondrous sight.
In the stillness, hearts align,
With echoes of the pure divine.

Crisp air holds a hush profound,
As weary souls seek common ground.
In the shadows, warmth will find,
A melody in hearts entwined.

As dawn breaks with a golden ray,
The whispers turn to bright display.
In winter's grasp, we feel anew,
The echoes wrapped in love's soft hue.

Shimmering Spirits in Wintry Air

In the twilight, spirits rise,
Dancing softly 'neath the skies.
Shimmering like the flakes that fall,
Whispers of a distant call.

They twirl and spin with grace untold,
Stories woven in threads of gold.
In the crispness of the night,
Their laughter sparkles, pure delight.

Moonlit shadows weave and weave,
Telling tales we long believe.
Each glimmer holds a memory tight,
Of moments bright, lost in light.

Among the trees and drifting snow,
The spirits dance, a gentle flow.
In their shimmer, dreams take flight,
Underneath the starlit night.

As dawn approaches, they fade away,
Yet in our hearts, they seem to stay.
For in the chill of winter air,
The shimmering spirits linger there.

Whispers of the Icy Veil

In the hush of frosty air,
Silent secrets drift with care.
Nature's breath, a ghostly sigh,
Whispers float beneath the sky.

Pines adorned with icy lace,
Glisten softly, time's embrace.
Footsteps crunch on snow's cold crust,
Echoes fade, in peace we trust.

Moonlight bathes the world in white,
Shadows dance with pure delight.
Stars above, a distant spark,
Guide us through the frozen dark.

Every flake, a tale untold,
Stories in the silence cold.
Winter's charm wrapped in a shroud,
Beauty whispered soft and proud.

In this realm where stillness reigns,
Find the warmth despite the chains.
Hearts ignite with quiet thrill,
In the whispers of the chill.

Starlit Chill of the Night

Beneath a canvas, dark and deep,
Stars awaken from their sleep.
Nighttime's breath, a chilling swell,
Dreams emerge where shadows dwell.

Every twinkle, a distant fire,
Lifts the heart and sparks desire.
Lonely paths beneath their glow,
Guide us where the spirits flow.

Frosty winds in whispers carry,
Secrets of the night to tarry.
In this stillness we connect,
With the universe in twilight's vest.

A silver beam, a gentle touch,
Wrapping us in calmness much.
Midnight's song, a soothing balm,
In the stillness, find the calm.

Each moment, precious, softly bright,
Cradled in the starlit night.
With each breath, we feel the thrill,
Of the chill that peace instills.

Shimmers in the Moonlit Mist

Veils of fog, a haunting sight,
Drape the world in silver light.
Mystic forms take shape and flow,
Whispers of the night bestow.

Candle glow from windows warm,
Sparks of life amidst the calm.
Each step taken with quiet grace,
Guided by the moon's soft face.

Pale beams splash on dampened ground,
Echoing the night's profound.
Gentle ripples through the trees,
Rustling softly with the breeze.

As shadows play in muted hues,
Nature shares its silent views.
Every shimmer, every mist,
Contains a magic not to miss.

In this dance of light and shade,
Wonder lingers, fears soon fade.
Moonlit paths, a tranquil bliss,
Found in shimmers of the mist.

Glacial Serenades of the Night

Under the frost, the whispers weave,
Songs of the night, in the air they cleave.
Moonlight dances on icy streams,
While shadows flicker, lost in dreams.

Silent stars in the velvet sky,
Guard the secrets, as they pass by.
Cold winds murmur through silver trees,
Echoes of time caught in the freeze.

The world rests beneath a crystal sheet,
Each glimmering fragment a heartbeat's beat.
In the stillness, a melody swells,
As nature's symphony softly dwells.

Frosty breath paints the air so light,
While darkness cloaks the lingering sight.
Serenades rise, interlaced and bold,
A tale of winter's enchantment told.

As dawn approaches, the chill remains,
In glacial serenades, life still sustains.
We hold in our hearts this sacred night,
Forever warmed by the ethereal light.

Reflections in the Frosted Twilight

Dusk settles down with a murmured sigh,
Frosted whispers begin to fly.
The world is cloaked in softest white,
As twilight weaves through the fading light.

Mirrored in stillness, the trees stand tall,
Crystals shimmering, answering the call.
Each breath a cloud in this tranquil scene,
Frosted twilight, a pureness serene.

Soft shadows dance in the fading glow,
As secrets of winter gently flow.
Past and present in silence entwine,
Reflections of memories, forever divine.

The hush of night, like a velvet shroud,
Wraps the earth in a gentle cloud.
With every heartbeat, the twilight sings,
A song of solace that winter brings.

In twilight's embrace, the beauty blooms,
Under the watch of silvered moons.
We linger here, hearts fated to be,
In reflections made of eternity.

The Stillness of a Frozen Heart

In a world where silence reigns supreme,
Frozen hearts hold the softest dream.
Time stands still in the icy air,
Whispers echo as if in prayer.

Beneath the frost, a warmth remains,
Fleeting shadows of love's refrains.
Frost-kissed hopes in the chilled embrace,
The stillness carved upon each trace.

In the quiet, the pulse does beat,
Like a secret hidden beneath the sheet.
Moments linger in the frozen light,
Painting stories within the night.

Each glimmer reflects an unspoken vow,
A promise held in the here and now.
Frozen hearts, though encased in cold,
Harbor warmth in the tales they hold.

As dawn breaks, the stillness fades,
Yet the memories in frost still wade.
In the heart's frozen, silent art,
Lies a warmth that shall never part.

Frost-kissed Memories Under the Stars

Amidst the frost, old stories cling,
Beneath the stars, they start to sing.
Each icy breath recalls the past,
Moments captured, forever cast.

Hearts wrapped tightly in winter's embrace,
Frost-kissed dreams, lined with grace.
Glistening thoughts in the night unfold,
Whispers of warmth never growing cold.

Under the cosmos, the night holds sway,
Guiding the lost who've lost their way.
In shimmering depths, memories glint,
A tapestry woven with time's own tint.

Frozen laughter lingers in air,
A world of wonders beyond compare.
Each shining star, a beacon bright,
Illuminates the depths of the night.

So we gather 'neath this heavenly dome,
Frost-kissed memories guiding us home.
In the chill, we find our warmth anew,
Under the stars, where dreams come true.

Enchantment Beneath a Silver Sky

In twilight's glow, the magic sings,
A world awash in silvery light.
Whispers of dreams take to the wings,
As stars awaken, shimmering bright.

Beneath the trees, shadows dance,
A gentle breeze stirs the air.
In this realm, all souls find chance,
To weave their stories, free of care.

A silver moon casts its sweet charm,
Painting the earth with a tender kiss.
Here, in this spell, there's no alarm,
Just hearts united in quiet bliss.

Each moment glows, time stands still,
As night unfolds its velvet lace.
In this embrace, we find a thrill,
Forever held in starlit grace.

Together we roam, hand in hand,
Through magic lands where dreams ignite.
In enchantment's realm, we take a stand,
Beneath the silver sky's soft light.

Chilling Dreams of Frozen Time

In the stillness, whispers creep,
As shadows clutch the frosty air.
Dreams of winter's hold, we keep,
In the silence, a world laid bare.

The moonlight spills on icy streams,
Where time seems to halt, to hold its breath.
Wrapped in chilling, sparkling beams,
A dance with echoes, life and death.

Snowflakes waltz with quiet grace,
Each crystalline flake, a tale to tell.
In frozen realms, we find our place,
In dreams where night and memory dwell.

Footprints fade on the snow's white sheet,
A fleeting trace of our soft flight.
Within these moments, hearts can meet,
And find their warmth in the biting night.

Embrace the cold, the frozen rhyme,
As we wander through this crystalline dome.
In the chilling dreams of frozen time,
We discover the beauty of coming home.

Ethereal Veil of the Twilight Hour

As day surrenders to twilight's sigh,
The world dons an ethereal veil.
Colors blend in the softening sky,
Whispers of dusk telling a tale.

A hush descends like a gentle shroud,
Embracing the earth in a tender hug.
Among the shadows, life feels proud,
As stars emerge, a celestial drug.

In this enchanted, fleeting space,
Time dances lightly, fleeting, yet bold.
Moments linger, a tender embrace,
As day's bright warmth turns to evening's cold.

Voices of night sing a soothing tune,
As dreams awaken beneath their glow.
In the stillness, under the moon,
We find the magic in every shadow.

With hearts alight in twilight's charms,
We cherish the beauty, the soft, the sweet.
In this ethereal veil that warms,
The sunset hues never know defeat.

Frosted Echoes in the Stillness

In the stillness, echoes ring clear,
Frosted whispers of what has been.
Each breath a sigh that draws us near,
To the quiet realms where we've seen.

Luminous crystals adorn the night,
Their glittering grace a sight to behold.
Frozen memories, pure and bright,
In the silence, their stories unfold.

Beneath the frost, the earth does sleep,
Protected by winter's soft embrace.
In this moment, we pause and weep,
For the beauty we cannot replace.

Time drifts gently, like snowflakes fall,
We gather moments held in the freeze.
In frosted echoes, we find it all,
In the stillness, our hearts find peace.

A world reborn in icy splendor,
Where echoes of life whisper sweet.
In this solitude, hearts tender,
Find solace in the soft heartbeat.

Riddles of Ice in the Darkened Woods

In shadows deep, secrets confide,
Whispers of frost, the night's silent guide.
Branches draped in a crystalline lace,
Nature's riddle, a frozen embrace.

Moonlight dances on shimmering streams,
Echoes of winter in half-formed dreams.
Each step taken, a crackling sound,
Footfalls lost in the magic all around.

Cold winds carry the tales of the night,
A spiral of silence, a flicker of light.
Figures emerge from the blanket of gleam,
Ghosts of the woods wrapped in snow's tender dream.

The air thickens, each breath turned to mist,
Frosty enchantments we cannot resist.
Here in these woods, the heart starts to race,
Riddles of ice, hidden treasures to trace.

In the embrace of chill, we are bound,
Under the stars, no noise can be found.
Each shattered shard sings a tune not yet heard,
Voices of winter, so distant, absurd.

Celestial Frost on Whispering Winds

Stars sprinkle frost on a velvet sky,
Whispers of night weave a lullaby.
Chilling the edges of dreams on the rise,
Celestial wonders, where silence lies.

Breezes carry secrets of frosty delight,
Painting the world in silvered light.
Each sigh of winter, a tender refrain,
Songs of the cosmos, laced with cold rain.

Glittering paths lead through time's soft embrace,
Dancing with shadows, the stars leave their trace.
In this stillness, hearts gather near,
Frost on the wind whispers, "You are here."

Beneath the vast canopy, breath turns to ice,
Echoes of laughter linger, so nice.
The universe spins in its delicate dance,
Celestial frost brings a dreamlike trance.

With every gust, a story unfolds,
The winds carry fragments of tales yet told.
In this frosted chapel of nature's grace,
We find our footing, our rightful place.

The Resonation of Quiet Chill

In the stillness, a shiver runs deep,
Resonating echoes, the forest's soft sweep.
Quiet chill speaks in a language so old,
Whispers of winter, both gentle and bold.

A tapestry woven from silence and air,
Threads of the coolness, a delicate flair.
Each breath we take, a frost-laden sigh,
Under the canopy, the world drifts by.

Ghostly figures drift through the frozen terrain,
Chasing the shadows, where beauty remains.
Nature's own heartbeat, so quiet, so clear,
The resonation beckons us near.

Underneath stars, the chill brings us peace,
With every tingle, our worries release.
In the hush of the night, a bond softly builds,
An orchestra played by the frost as it spills.

Together we stand in the ambient glow,
Wrapped in the whispers of flurries of snow.
In the quiet chill, we discover a spark,
Unity found in the darkened arc.

An Alchemy of Ice and Dream

In twilight's grasp, where the dreams intertwine,
Ice weaves a story, ancient and fine.
Glistening visions, a tapestry spun,
An alchemy of frost, where all things are one.

Each crystal shimmering, a fragment of light,
A whispering promise that dances so bright.
In the realm of the cold, our spirits take flight,
Embracing the magic that cloaks us in white.

Under the sheen of an argent embrace,
Possibilities shimmer in this frozen space.
Where time loses grip and the heart learns to dream,
An alchemy brewing, as rare as a beam.

Hands of the night mold the ice into form,
Creating a haven, a sanctuary warm.
In the stillness, we delve into realms unconfined,
An alchemy stirring, our visions aligned.

As dawn threatens day with a blush of soft hue,
The dreams wrapped in ice bid a fond adieu.
Yet in the heart lingers each shimmering gleam,
An alchemy everlasting, in the wake of a dream.

The Silence of Shimmering Leaves

In the stillness of the grove,
Leaves whisper secrets soft and low,
Dancing gently in the light,
Shimmering with a golden glow.

Beneath the branches, shadows play,
Nature's breath, a quiet sigh,
The world stands still, in trance, it stays,
As fleeting moments flutter by.

Crimson hues and amber tones,
Wrap the trees like tender lace,
A symphony of autumn's moans,
In every rustle, time's embrace.

Golden sunlight filters through,
Casting patterns on the ground,
In this sanctuary, calm and true,
The beauty of the leaves is found.

As evening falls, the colors fade,
But memories linger on, so bright,
In the silence, dreams are made,
The leaves will dance again with night.

Celestial Chill in the Quiet Hour

When twilight drapes the world in blue,
A chill descends, serene and bold,
The stars awaken, fresh and new,
In whispers, ancient tales unfold.

The moon, a guardian in the dark,
Sinks low, casting silver threads,
Each glimmer forms a tranquil spark,
Where dreams take flight, and hope embeds.

Beneath the sky, the world lies hushed,
A canvas vast, in stillness framed,
As night unfolds, all worries brushed,
A cosmic lullaby proclaimed.

In this embrace of night and chill,
Time pauses, wrapped in endless rest,
Hearts awaken, and dreams fulfill,
In the quiet hour, we're blessed.

Only the wind, a soft caress,
Breathes life into the calm expanse,
In every moment, we possess,
The magic of this night's romance.

The Elegance of Winter's Grasp

As winter's breath, a gentle sigh,
Cloaks the earth in crystal white,
Each flake that falls, a lullaby,
An elegant dance in the fading light.

Trees adorned in frosty gowns,
Stand silent in their icy grace,
While nature weaves a quilt of crowns,
That glistens bright in cold embrace.

Footprints trace a story told,
In the snow, soft whispers cling,
A tapestry of dreams unfold,
As winter crowns the world a king.

The air, a crisp and biting new,
Brings warmth in hearths and laughter's glow,
In every breath, the chill rings true,
As night descends with stars aglow.

In this brief hush, the heart can soar,
With beauty wrapped in icy clasp,
Winter's elegance we can't ignore,
In each moment, we softly grasp.

Frosted Petals Underneath the Moon

In gardens where the shadows loom,
Frosted petals lay in rows,
Underneath the silver moon,
Nature's grace in still repose.

Delicate dreams in every bloom,
Whispers of the night set free,
A fragrant breath, a gentle plume,
In the quiet, they softly plea.

As frost clings tight while stars ignite,
Softly draped in winter's care,
Their colors fade, yet hold the light,
A silent promise, bold and rare.

Each petal kissed by icy breath,
Finds beauty in the darkened hour,
Life's resilience, even in death,
A testament to nature's power.

The moon keeps watch, a guardian bright,
As dreams are woven, soft and slow,
In this dance of dark and light,
Frosted petals bid us glow.

The Dance of Chill and Stars

In the quiet night sky,
Stars waltz with the moon's glow,
A chill whispers through trees,
Nature's breath, soft and slow.

Footprints crunch on the ground,
Each step a story told,
As frost embraces the earth,
In a shroud of silver and gold.

The air, crisp like a sigh,
Draws dreams into the night,
Upon the frosted air,
A shimmering delight.

Beneath the celestial dome,
Hearts sway to the refrain,
Of winter's gentle pulse,
A dance in frozen vein.

In the stillness, we find,
A harmony so rare,
The chill and stars entwined,
In a cosmic, tender stare.

Shards of Light on Frosted Glass

Morning breaks with soft rays,
Kissing frost upon the pane,
Shards of light scatter gently,
Creating a sparkling chain.

Each droplet, a tiny gem,
Reflecting the world outside,
A dance of color and form,
In beauty, we take in stride.

The warmth begins to rise,
Yet frost still holds its reign,
Whispers of winter's grip,
In a delicate domain.

Through the shards, visions bloom,
Life's stories yet untold,
Captured in glimmers bright,
In the morning's embrace, bold.

As sunlight weaves its thread,
Through crystals of frosted grace,
We find our hearts alight,
In this shimmering embrace.

Nocturnal Lace in the Heart of Winter

Underneath the moon's gaze,
Night weaves a delicate lace,
Frost patterns on bare branches,
In the winter's cold embrace.

Silent whispers fill the air,
With each breath, a world anew,
Stars sprinkle tales of old,
In shadows, they softly strew.

The chill wraps around us tight,
A cloak of stillness and peace,
In the heart of winter's night,
All worries seem to cease.

Snowflakes dance down like dreams,
Caught in a magical waltz,
Nature's artistry unfolds,
In the silence, love exalts.

As the moonlight leads the way,
Through a realm of soft delight,
Nocturnal lace, a blessing,
In the depths of endless night.

A Serenade for Shimmering Nights

Under the blanket of dark,
Stars twinkle like distant flames,
A serenade softly plays,
In the quiet, no one claims.

Snowflakes swirl in their flight,
Glistening under the glow,
Each flurry, a note of joy,
In the chill, they twirl and flow.

The breeze carries sweet wishes,
As whispers of dreams collide,
In the night, our hopes gather,
In the silence, they confide.

A chorus of crickets sings,
Nature's night symphony bright,
In the arms of winter's song,
We find solace in the light.

As the world slows to a hush,
And stars weave their gentle spell,
We dance in the shimmering dark,
Where the heart's true stories dwell.

An Ode to Winter's Silent Embrace

The snow falls soft upon the ground,
A quilt of white, a hushed surround.
Whispers dance on icy breath,
Embracing all in winter's caress.

Trees stand tall, their branches bare,
Draped in frost, a glistening wear.
Each step cracks in frozen bliss,
A tranquil moment, a winter's kiss.

The world is still, time held at bay,
As twilight fades to end the day.
Stars emerge, a twinkling rune,
Beneath the glow of a silver moon.

Fires flicker in cozy nooks,
While outside, silence softly looks.
In this peace, the heart finds grace,
An ode to winter's silent embrace.

So let us cherish every chill,
The quiet calm, the throbbing thrill.
For in this season, we find our way,
In winter's heart, we choose to stay.

Silver Dreams Beneath a Frozen Canopy

In stillness wrapped, the night unfolds,
Beneath a canopy, silver and cold.
Stars twinkle like dreams afar,
Guiding paths where wishes are.

Silent glades, where whispers play,
The breath of night, a soft ballet.
Moonlit branches sway and bend,
Nature's magic, a gentle trend.

The frost-kissed ground, a sparkling sight,
With each step, hearts take flight.
Dreams awaken in this frozen land,
A realm of wonder, beautifully planned.

In each flake, a story spun,
Of icy warmth, and gentle fun.
Silver dreams that softly gleam,
Underneath this frozen theme.

A dance of shadows, light and dark,
Nature's canvas, each brush a spark.
In the whispering wind, we find release,
Silver dreams bring forth sweet peace.

The Poetry of Ice and Starshine

Upon the pond, a still expanse,
The stars above begin to dance.
Reflections mirror the night's embrace,
A tapestry of time and space.

Each breath a cloud, the world is bright,
In frozen still, we find our light.
The poetry of ice, so clear,
Whispers secrets for all to hear.

With every sparkle, stories rise,
Underneath the vast, starlit skies.
Nature writes in crystals fine,
An elegy of frost divine.

In shadows cast by the moon's glow,
Dreams ignite, like fireflies flow.
With quiet grace, the night unfolds,
The poetry of ice, a tale retold.

So let us wander, hand in hand,
Through this enchanted, glorious land.
For in each glimmer, hope is found,
In ice and starshine, joy abounds.

Ethereal Whispers from the Frozen Woods

Deep in the woods, where silence reigns,
Ethereal whispers flow like chains.
Amid the trees, a world of light,
Wrapped in snow, pure and bright.

The crunch of boots on crystal crust,
Echoes softly, beneath the trust.
In solitude, the heart takes flight,
Finding solace in winter's night.

Shadows dance on the frosty ground,
In every corner, wonders found.
Nature's voice, a subtle sound,
In frozen woods, where dreams abound.

Snowflakes twirl on whispers' breath,
A gentle hymn, a song of death.
Yet life persists in frosty breath,
Amidst the ether, there's no theft.

So let the whispers guide us near,
Through frozen realms where hearts grow clear.
In winter's hush, we hear the call,
Ethereal whispers, inspiring all.

Milton Keynes UK
Ingram Content Group UK Ltd.
UKHW020700021224
3298UKWH00039B/306